NEW LENSES

52 Personal Challenges, Thoughts, and Convictions of a Humble Sinner

By: John F. Hendershot

People can change. You can change, and I can change, and that is the goal every day of my life – to work on the less desirable things about myself and become a better person. Go on a journey with me to transform your life for the better. Do-it for yourself, your family, and your loved ones. You are worth it – a perfect creation designed by a perfect creator. Let's go!

NEW LENSES

52 Personal Challenges, Thoughts, and Convictions of a Humble Sinner

By: John F. Hendershot

*DISCLAIMER: This book is not geared towards academics, so if it's not sophisticated enough for your taste – that's okay. I write in the same vernacular in which I speak --- NORMAL. If you are looking for something boring that will not challenge you – pick another book. This book is for those of us that are broken, humbled, and open to new possibilities for our lives. Enjoy.

NEW LENSES

52 Personal Challenges, Thoughts, and Convictions of a Humble Sinner

Dedicated to:

My children, Courtland, Alivia, and Reagan as well as their cousins Lexi, Isabella, Marley, Ethan, Isaiah, Lilian, Ava, Aidan, Lily, Annabelle, and Cayden.

A <u>VERY</u> special thanks to the love of my life, my beautiful wife Rachel. Thank you for being patient with me, and giving me a chance.

I want to give a special acknowledgement to my son Courtland, who graduates from high school this year and embarks on a new chapter of life. You are a true blessing. A joy to my heart. Keep dreaming and believing in yourself, because you are the perfect handiwork of God our Creator. Thank you for being who you are, I am so proud of the young man that you have become. I love you.

-Dad

Change is possible. You can do it!

*Note: Before we begin, allow me to offer you a few quick tips on how to have the richest possible experience in reading this book.

1. Give it Time – I want to challenge you to read one chapter a week. I understand that the book is short, but the point is that this is an exercise to challenge you mentally and spiritually.

2. Write stuff down! - What comes to mind when you read each chapter? How does it make you feel? Are you challenged by the chapter? Is there anything in your life that needs altering?

Use the WHITESPACE – There is purposely a lot of blank space throughout this book. Use it!

3. Relax – Even though it may only take a couple minutes to read each chapter STOP, SIT, RELAX, and really think about YOURSELF and what challenges you personally.

Thank you in advance for reading my thoughts. I hope you are challenged by them and strive to become better every day as I do. Please feel free to use this book among peer groups and small groups, too. Respect yourself and others, and live a life full of love and joy. -JFH

Introduction

Most of us have stumbled, fallen, messed up, and made serious mistakes in our lives. The most important thing we can do is try and stand up, brush our knees off — and strive to right our wrongs and lead a better life moving forward.

I believe that everyone is redeemable, because of the miraculous gift of forgiveness through Christ Jesus. Nevertheless, throughout this process it is necessary for us to begin refining ourselves by developing new ways of thinking and unlearning unhealthy habits.

You matter. Your life matters. You are a gift perfectly created by the master architect. There are situations and people in our lives that have caused us to question that, but they are wrong! You are valuable! You are wonderful! And you deserve to take the opportunity to work on yourself to become a better person every day.

Don't give up on yourself. You are phenomenal!

In the Beginning

Where does your thinking come from? Does it elevate you or hold you back? Where does your motivation come from? Is it self-serving or serving someone? What is life-giving to you? What brings you joy and gives you peace?

These are some of the most important questions that you must ask yourself in order to grow and prosper into the calling that you were meant to live. Life isn't about yesterday or tomorrow, but instead about what you are doing TODAY to become the best person you were created to be.

Are you frustrated because of the untapped potential you have? Maybe that's because you aren't challenging yourself enough. To truly experience who you were created to be, you have to be willing to intentionally challenge your thinking and how you view the world. This is very difficult, because most of our daily interactions don't feel very intentional. We've developed passive habits like small talk, watching television or surfing the web that don't teach us anything meaningful about ourselves, each other, or the world. More and more, our interactions tend to be about nothing, causing the fire in each of us to become nothing more that smoke.

Why is it that we seem to stumble around in life, not living, but watching the unrenewable commodity of time pass through our fingers? Could it be that we are lazy? I am not talking about physical laziness (which could be the case), but mental laziness. Does life just happen to you? Is it always someone else's fault? Do you think the world is conspiring against you?

When we get to points like this in our life, are we asking questions such as, what can I do to...? What am I learning in going through this difficult period of my life?

My friend, life is a journey. A journey that might not allow you to reach your destination for a very long time. A journey that is going to be cold, wet, hot, dry, hilly and even at times mountainous. Along the way, take the time to experience the beauty, decadence, and majesty of where you are and where you came from. We only get one chance at the journey. It is kind of like starting a PAC MAN game with your last life remaining. How can I make it count? How can I leave a legacy worth writing about? What can I do to make _____ proud of me?

Throughout my life I have learned quite a few lessons, some the hard way, others observed from a safe distance. I was born in a small south central Ohio town that was on the cusp of Appalachia. I literally lived three houses down from the train tracks, but it honestly did not matter which side of the tracks that you lived on, because neither was better than the other. My parents worked hard, and I was blessed with a great family, but I always felt like there was much more to life. For as long as I can remember, I have wanted to be an advocate for positive change in the world, whether it's helping the less fortunate, sharing financial expertise, growing a business to be able to offer more opportunities to my team members, or encouraging people to grow through knowledge, training, and discipline.

The lessons below are not the only ones that are important to learn in this life. They are simply the lessons that have taught me throughout my own journey, and I hope they help you as you seek to become a fully-engaged, active, and humble participant in life.

Do you wish to rise? Begin by descending. You plan a tower that will pierce the clouds? Lay first the foundation of humility.

-Saint Augustine

Week #1 Humility

Humility is one of the most important characteristics that any of us can possess. Innately, we are all vulnerable in different ways, but that doesn't mean we are weak. Instead, there is "power" in being vulnerable because it allows us to be able to connect at a deeper level with people. Conversely, if we lack humility and think ourselves as being better than others, then we miss a great opportunity to fully bond on a deep level with one another.

What does humility look like? Well let me begin first by stating what humility is not. Humility is not weakness; it is not some frumpy hunch-back man that gets picked on, laughed at, and taken advantage of. Instead, humility means intentionally forsaking your selfishness and putting another person's interests before yours. That can take many forms, such as giving your time, teaching, mentoring or coming alongside of someone.

Things to Consider: Before you can effectively lead a team, a club, a family, a department, a business, or a church, you must be able to meet the needs of those you are leading and submit to elevating them (the team/ group) as your primary goal.

The Bible on Humility: "Then He poured water into the basin, and began to wash the disciples' feet and to wipe them with the towel with which He was girded." John 13:5

Would you ever get down on your knees and wash someone's dirty sandal-wearing feet? Think about that—stinky, sweaty, dirty feet. Jesus got down on his knees and washed every single one of his disciple's feet. That is certainly a great example of humility. What are some steps that you can take in exercising that level of humility in your own life?

Silence is a source of great strength. -Lao Tzu

Week #2 Silence

Do you ever partake in acts like driving, walking, sitting, or others where you are in a prolonged state of silence? In a heavily-charged, plugged-in society, it can be challenging to turn off the noise and distractions in our everyday life.

Silence was always a tough practice for me to be committed to, and truthfully it can still be a bit of a daily challenge for me. But I find that the benefits of allowing myself to be silent without any distractions can be quite relaxing, energizing and contemplative.

Things to Consider: Life is busy, the world around us is moving at warp speed. When we are sleeping and unconscious our body is being recharged to begin a new day. Consider silence in that same way, except you are conscious. Our breathing is relaxed, there are no distractions; this too is life-giving and energizes us to go back into the noisy world.

The Bible on Silence: "Even a fool, when he keeps silent, is considered wise; When he closes his lips, he is considered prudent." Proverbs 17:28

Forefather wisdom: In Benjamin Franklin's Lessons in Manliness: Benjamin Franklin's Pursuit of a Virtuous Life, Mr. Franklin states "Speak not but what may benefit others or yourself; avoid trifling conversation."

The only true wisdom is in knowing you know nothing -
Socrates

Week #3 Wisdom

Wisdom is something most people get wrong. I believe that wisdom is sometimes or even many times gained through foolish acts. We do something stupid, we feel guilty, we ask for forgiveness, and through that process we expanded our wisdom basin.

I know for myself, when someone asks me about wise individuals I think of King Solomon, who God called the wisest man to ever live. Solomon wasn't wise because he never made any mistakes. On the contrary, he made many mistakes in his pursuit of knowledge, to the point that he even counted his vast fortune as worthless.

What mistakes have you made that have given you insight? What have you learned? How can these mistakes guide your future?

Things to Consider: Since Adam and Eve in the garden of Eden EVERYONE has made mistakes. Some mistakes may have greater consequences than others, but regardless we have all made mistakes. The challenge for you is, is your life going to be defined by your or another's mistake, or at this moment are you going to choose to become wiser and not repeat the mistakes of the past?

The Bible on Wisdom: "And Joshua the son of Nun was full of the spirit of wisdom; for Moses had laid his hands upon him: and the children of Israel hearkened unto him, and did as the LORD commanded Moses." Deut. 34:9

The weak can never forgive. Forgiveness is the attribute of the strong. -Mahatma Gandhi

Week #4 Forgiveness

Have you been wronged in life? Taken advantage of? Hurt? Made fun of? Life can be harsh, downright discouraging, and sometimes unfair. Chances are that most, if not all of us, have from one time or another experienced pain, hurt, trauma, or anguish.

Your pain is real, don't discount that. But we tend to realize that the pain consumes us so much that it seems to handicap our lives, and therefore never lets us move on from the pain. To grant yourself peace you must be able to forgive the person who offended you. That doesn't diminish what they did, but instead frees you from the burden you have been carrying.

Things to Consider: There are two scenarios I have experienced in life. The first was that the person who offended me did not realize what they did and was clueless that I was even offended, and the second was that the person who offended me has been racked with guilt for years over the offense.

The Bible on Forgiveness: "For if you let men have forgiveness for their sins, you will have forgiveness from your Father in heaven." Matthew 6:14

How poor are they that have not patience! What wound did ever heal but by degrees? -William Shakespeare

Change is possible. You can do it!

Week #5 Patience

Patience is one of the most difficult characteristics for myself to exhibit. I am the type of person that would complete todays work last week, because I am naturally adversarial towards being patient. I am certain that patience is a trait that begins being formed in us when we are young, and how necessary it is to those in leadership positions in how we react and test ourselves in our patience.

I have learned that if we fail to exhibit patience then we end up settling in life with options and opportunities that we should have passed on. A couple of examples that may seem trite, choosing the speediness of a fast food restaurant over the healthier option of packing our lunch. Or how about purchasing something at a very high price instead of exhibiting patience and evaluating your options and doing research.

The fact is, that at one point or another we have all been remorseful about an impulsive decision that we have made, and wish that we could turn back the clock. Unfortunately, none of us can jump into a time machine and alter our decisions.

Something to Consider: Think about something that you currently do, or have done in your life that lacks patience. What is it? Write them down. Set a game plan; a goal of sorts. Begin to hold yourself accountable. Eventually, if you are serious about changing, and put forth a serious-minded effort you will begin to see yourself becoming more patient.

The Bible on Patience: "Now the God of patience and consolation grant you to be likeminded one toward another according to Christ Jesus. "Romans 15:5

Whether one believes in a religion or not, and whether one believes in rebirth or not, there isn't anyone who doesn't appreciate kindness and compassion. -Dalai Lama

Week #6 Kindness

Have you ever been somewhere that is foreign to you? Or prodded to step outside of your comfort zone to pursue something that you lacked confidence in? Does it warm your heart when someone you don't know puts themselves in an uncomfortable position to ensure that you were welcome, encouraged, and made to feel at ease?

I know that whenever I am somewhere new or seeking an opportunity that may be uncomfortable for me, I become more relaxed when someone reaches out to me in a non-threatening manner.

We as humankind have a great assignment in transforming our culture for a positive benefit, and what is more transformational and positive than giving kindness to or receiving kindness from everyone you meet? Think about the difference our world would experience if we constantly lived our lives in a state of kindness. I know that this sounds like a utopian dream, but what if we could bring a little bit of that utopia into reality bit by bit every day?

Things to Consider: Most everyone has heard of the concept of random acts of kindness, and some communities have run campaigns built around this concept to encourage people "paying-forward" the kindness.

Have you demonstrated kindness recently? How about to a stranger? Better yet, how about to someone that you can gain nothing in return from?

The Bible on Kindness: "Do not forget or neglect to do kindness and good, to be generous and distribute and contribute to the needy [of the church as embodiment and proof of fellowship], for such sacrifices are pleasing to God." Hebrews 13:16

Love is the only force capable of transforming an enemy into a friend. -Martin Luther King, Jr.

Week #7 Love

Who knows the Beatles song "All You Need is Love"? Love is arguably the most important characteristic that one can possess. Unfortunately, society has discolored and falsified what love is, and how the narrative should play out.

First, love is not what you see in the "movies". And unfortunately, even though movies can be entertaining they create false expectations and make it nearly impossible for any of us to live up to a Hollywood script. Second, love is not lust. Magazines, romance novels, and other types of medias pollute our minds and trick our emotions into thinking that sex, sexiness, and other forms of expressing love are indeed love, but they are not.

Love is a form of expression about who we are. Love is a heart condition that is not predicated on emotions, but instead on a person's choice of being. Loving someone is not based on attractiveness or what you can get from them. On the contrary, it is a conscious decision to be with them through good and bad.

Something to Consider: If love is not an emotion or about what we can gain, what is it to you? How can you radiate love and make it a choice you partake in daily? What positive benefits can you see in your life in doing so? What does this look like in practice?

The Bible on Love: "And above all these put on love, which binds everything together in perfect harmony." Colossians 3:14

Nothing is more noble, nothing more venerable than fidelity. Faithfulness and truth are the most sacred excellences and endowments of the human mind. -Marcus Tullius Cicero

Week #8 Faithfulness

What does faithfulness mean to you? If you do not consider yourself a faith-based person, do you believe that faithfulness can provide any benefit to your life?

I believe that faithfulness is a state of who we are. It is an inherent part of our character whether or not we gravitate toward a specific religion. People are "faithful" in many ways: to their spouse, children, parents, a non-profit, vocation, etc. However, my faithfulness in all areas of my life is guided by my spiritual faith. My faith in Jesus Christ enables me to be faithful in the other parts of my life. I believe that my closeness or faithfulness to the word of Jesus also dictates how faithful I am being throughout my entire existence.

Faithfulness is about what you are honoring or dedicating your life to. Why are we on this earth, and what are we supposed to do with the time that we are given? If we are not faithful to something other than our selfish desires, then we are missing out on what life is truly about. I don't think the short span of time we are given from birth to death is supposed to be about us, but about devoting ourselves to something bigger, something that has meaning, something that transcends our lives.

Things to Consider: Our days on the earth are numbered. Unfortunately, we wake up every day with one less day in our basket. What defines your life? What are you living for? What is the legacy that you want to outlive you?

The Bible on Faithfulness: "Do not let anyone look down on you because you are young, but be an example for other believers in your speech, behavior, love, faithfulness, and purity." 1 Timothy 4:12

The value of a promise is the cost to you of keeping your word.
-Brian Tracy

Week #9 Truth / Keeping Your Word

It was once said that a "man's word was his bond", and with that a handshake was a consummation of an agreement between parties. Unfortunately, that is no longer the case in many circumstances, and these days an agreement is buttressed by massive documents with clauses that can nullify the agreement if not met.

I believe that a person's word should still be honored to the best of their ability. I understand that there are situational circumstances that make it complicated to make your word a black and white issue, but the reality is that the better we are at keeping our word, the more people will trust us and want to conduct life and do business with us.

With all intent on being fair to this topic, it goes with saying that "Truth" cannot be subjective, but instead must be based on concrete facts. Therefore, if I agree to an arrangement with someone and we shake hands over it, it becomes a truth and each party is obligated to keep their word.

Things to Consider: We live in a society where truth or keeping one's word has become simply just hot air. What if we limited our agreements to give credence to the obligations that we have already established? Would doing so, negate the futility of one's word? Consider for a moment how much disappointment you would avert if you always told the truth and honored your word. Do you think that maybe you might reduce complications that you may currently be experiencing?

The Bible on Truth/ Keeping Your Word: "If you make a vow to the LORD your God, do not be slow to pay it, for the LORD your God will certainly demand it of you and you will be guilty of sin. But if you refrain from vowing, you will not be guilty of sin." Deuteronomy 23:21-22

These men ask for just the same thing, fairness, and fairness only.
This, so far as in my power, they, and all others, shall have.

-Abraham Lincoln

Change is possible. You can do it!

Week #10: Fairness

Wouldn't the world be a better place if we were more fair with everyone we met? The truth of the matter is that the world is not fair. Most of the seven billion people that populate the earth are subjected to harsh environments, lack safety resources, malnourishment, substandard medical care, and extreme poverty.

Without any choice of our own, many of us have been granted the opportunity to flourish in a society that is filled with great abundance. We can choose to be consumed with all that we have or we can set out to become more fair and generous in every aspect of our lives.

The unfortunate reality is that we tend to judge others based on their economic circumstances, religion, language barrier, educational level, or cultural or racial differences. In doing so, we miss the opportunity to connect at a deeper level with them because we did not allow ourselves to act fairly toward them. Think about all the times in our lives where we forfeited the opportunity to give hope, guidance, or assistance to someone in need.

Things to Consider: What if we treated people who were different than we are the same way we treat our close friends? Do you think that a transformation of our minds and how we see the sacred humanity in everyone would start to take shape?

The Bible on Fairness: "There is neither Jew nor Greek, there is neither slave nor free, there is no male and female, for you are all one in Christ Jesus." Galatians 3:28

You will not be punished for your anger; you will be punished by your anger. -Buddha

Week #11 Anger

There is truly no greater joy killer than anger. Many of us only deal with small bursts of anger, while others struggle with it constantly. Anger is a form of frustration that takes hold of our entire being and zaps any display of goodness in us. That is not to say that anger is not warranted in any circumstance. Naturally we should be angered about injustices, atrocities, and devastating effects on humanity.

However, the problem with anger comes when it is not controlled and manifested in a healthy way. When we choose not to exercise discretion and instead allow our anger to dictate our behavior, we often make mistakes that can be embarrassing or even devastating. But whether you are left with guilt, embarrassment or both, succumbing to anger can lead to a tarnished reputation and can inflict severe damage to a relationship.

Things to Consider: How does it make you feel when someone displays anger toward you or perhaps just in your presence? Does it make you anxious, hurt, worried, or scared? In turn, think of those that you have directed your anger towards. How do you think they felt?

The Bible on Anger: "Whoever is slow to anger has great understanding, but he who has a hasty temper exalts folly." Proverbs 14:29

Over time, grit is what separates fruitful lives from aimlessness.

-John Ortberg

Week #12 Fruitfulness

The Bible often talks about our works being the outward expression of our faith, and Jesus explains this in the same way fruit on a vine takes form. So, if the stages of growing fruit are like the various stages of growth and maturity that each of us experience, what type of fruit are we bringing forth?

I believe that fruitfulness is the culmination of all the virtues that make us able to accomplish the mission we were called to pursue. To break this down further, being fruitful may look different for each of us throughout different stages of our lives.

So, whatever you were called to do at this time in your life, do it with everything positive that you have in you, and to the best of your ability.

Things to Consider: What if everything that we did, we did it to the best of our ability? What if we didn't hold back on striving for our best in everything that we did? How do you think that this might positively affect your life?

If you are doing something half-heartedly, STOP. Why are you even trying? Let it go and focus on something that you are going to give everything you got. Don't be lazy!

The Bible on Fruitfulness: "I am the true vine, and my Father is the vinedresser. Every branch in me that does not bear fruit he takes away, and every branch that does bear fruit he prunes, that it may bear more fruit. Already you are clean because of the word that I have spoken to you. Abide in me, and I in you. As the branch cannot bear fruit by itself, unless it abides in the vine, neither can you, unless you abide in me. I am the vine; you are the branches. Whoever abides in me and I in him, he it is that bears much fruit, for apart from me you can do nothing." John 15:1-5

You can change your world by changing your words... Remember, death and life are in the power of the tongue.   *-Joel Osteen*

Week: #13 The Tongue

The most powerful weapon you can wield is your tongue. I once heard that "our words were a window into our thoughts". Therefore, whatever we give our time and energy to will inevitably reveal itself at some point.

Harnessing our tongue can be like pulling back the reins on a Clydesdale horse. It is very difficult to stop, and nearly impossible to slow down once you get started. Therefore, we should be cautious about what we fill our minds with. If you fill your mind full of garbage, then garbage will tend to flow out of your mouth. The perfect example is using curse words. I tend to think that using such words are never effective, and in fact they give the appearance of a limited vocabulary or instability.

Things to Consider: What if you opened your mouth less? What if you stopped gossiping? What if you quit using curse or slang words? Do you think there would be any positive impact on your daily life?

The Bible on the tongue: "Whoever keeps his mouth and his tongue keeps himself out of trouble." Proverbs 21:23

Success is no accident. It is hard work, perseverance, learning, studying, sacrifice and most of all, love of what you are doing or learning to do. -Pele

Change is possible. You can do it!

Week #14 Perseverance

Most people chalk success up to luck, being gifted, or some other intangible thing. I believe success is highly correlated to our ability to persevere. Perseverance can take shape in many ways in our lives—school, a job, marriage, health issues, etc.—but what is at the core of perseverance is the will to keep trying and not give up.

I see life as a marathon, and throughout the race giving up is not an option. So, whether I am dealing with a relationship issue or a health issue there may need to be a lot of tough work involved. I believe that anything of value in this life is difficult, and by persevering through that difficulty you have discovered the great importance of it.

Things to Consider: Are there things in your life that you gave up on and wished you hadn't? When something gets tough, do you keep pursuing the goal?

The Bible on Perseverance: "Do you not know that in a race all the runners run, but only one receives the prize? So, run that you may obtain it. Every athlete exercises self-control in all things. They do it to receive a perishable wreath, but we an imperishable. So, I do not run aimlessly; I do not box as one beating the air. But I discipline my body and keep it under control, lest after preaching to others I myself should be disqualified." 1 Corinthians 9:24-27

I'm not concerned with your liking or disliking me... All I ask is that you respect me as a human being. -Jackie Robinson

Week #15 Respect

In both my business and personal interactions, I have been noticing a growing disregard of respect in our society. That seems to be a blanket statement, and it does not extend to everyone, but it seems to be happening more and more.

I hear people say, "I will respect them when they..." or "they don't deserve respect", and so on. I have become deeply saddened by this, because in the process, we end up denigrating positions and people who could garner our respect even if we disagree with them. In the absence of civil discourse, disrespect and even contempt have become commonplace, and those are two things that often provide the spark for violence and upheaval.

These acts are perpetuated by selfishness and an attempt to disrupt or prevent the opposition's voice. It should be extremely disturbing when we make those we disagree with out to be evil, instead of just having a different point of view.

An educated person should not be threatened by the views or beliefs of another. Regardless of our opinion or held beliefs, we should never disrespect anyone. Everyone should be afforded respect.

Things to Consider: What if we took time to honor and respect those in service positions? What if we tipped better? What if we paid for lunch for the civil servant catching a quick bite in the diner while they are on their beat? What if we held the door open for the elderly person, carried the groceries for the pregnant woman or even taught our kids to listen and obey in school?

What if we didn't teach our children that they are victims, and stood behind the school when they disciplined them? What if we became intentional about respecting everyone that we met? Can you imagine the changes that you would see in people?

The Bible on Respect: "So, whatever you wish that others would do to you, do also to them, for this is the Law and the Prophets." Matthew 7:22

"Love one another with brotherly affection. Outdo one another in showing honor." Romans 12:10

The meaning of life. The wasted years of life. The poor choices of life. God answers the mess of life with one word: 'grace.'
-Max Lucado

Week #16 Grace

Grace is like receiving a gift you never expected to receive. Have you ever bombed an opportunity that someone had given you, and afterward you felt like you didn't live up to the expectations of that person?

I know that I have. Not once, but probably more times than I can count. Grace is a gift that cannot be earned, but is freely given to us. It enables us to free ourselves from whatever the disappointment was.

We should live in a way that we would afford someone the same kind of grace that we would want to be afforded.

Things to Consider: If grace was offered freely to you, and you too offered grace freely, what type of radical change would you experience in your life?

The Bible on Grace: "But he gives more grace. Therefore, it says, 'God opposes the proud, but gives grace to the humble.'" James 4:6

Jesus alone cleanses from sin; He only can forgive our transgressions. -Ellen G. White

Change is possible. You can do it!

Week #17 Past Transgressions

The one thing that is certain for all of us is that we cannot go back and change the mistakes we have made in our lives. They are history. What we can do is learn from our mistakes, and develop a plan that allows us to move forward towards success.

It is important that you do not let your past define your present or your future. The unfortunate thing is that a lot of us get to a point in our lives when we want a better way of life. We want to put the things of our youth behind us, but we believe, falsely, that we are not good enough or capable of doing so. We believe that we cannot change or we would seem like a fraud, or we don't have the resources that we need to change.

These concerns are real, and the road to change will most likely be rocky, full of backsliding, and downright uncomfortable. But it is worth it. You owe it to yourself, your family, and your creator to finish this one and only life strong and on the right track.

Here are a couple first steps to assist you in getting started:

1. Get down on your knees and ask God to forgive you, and ask him to come alongside you though the remainder of the journey.

2. If you offended someone, ask for forgiveness.

3. Get help (counselor, or pastor).

4. Choose your circle wisely to prevent backsliding.

5. Begin to read the Bible (start in the New Testament in the gospel of Luke).

6. Get a mentor or accountability partner.

7. Write down your goals; figure out what you need to work on.

8. Find a church community to participate in.

9. Don't give up; stay faithful.

10. Give back with your time and talents.

Things to Consider: What if we truly repented from our sins and asked for forgiveness? Do you think we could become freed of the bonds that our past sins have locked us into?

The Bible on past transgressions: "If we confess our sins, he is faithful and just to forgive us our sins and to cleanse us from all unrighteousness." 1 John 1:9

A happy marriage is a long conversation which always seems too short. -Andre Maurois

Week #18 Marriage

Marriage has been the greatest experience of my life. Taking two immensely different individuals and blending them together to perform this beautiful ballet of a partnership is profoundly the greatest joy of my life.

Sure, marriage is tough, hard work, trying, frustrating, and just downright difficult at times. It tests the essence of who we are as individuals, and forces us to strip away negative characteristics like selfishness, greed, and complacency. To experience the glories of marriage, one must live a life dedicated to something far greater than the self.

There is nothing more satisfying than sharing life with someone who connects with you mentally, spiritually, physically, and emotionally. In fact, I see marriage as a prelude to what Heaven is going to be like.

Things to Consider: What if society as a whole honored its covenants and held marriage to the standard that it is meant to be? Would there be less poverty? Would there be more children being raised in two-parent homes with discipline?

The Bible on Marriage: "He who finds a wife finds a good thing and obtains favor from the LORD." Proverbs 18:22

A dream doesn't become reality through magic; it takes sweat, determination and hard work. -Colin Powell

Week #19 Work

The world will try to define you based upon the occupation that you choose. They will judge you based upon your work uniform, the amount of money that you make, the type of work that you do, and whether they believe what you do is a noble cause.

The occupation you have should not define your life purpose or calling. And while two could be inclusive, they do not have to be. What's more important is HOW you perform your job. In everything that you do, do it to the best of your ability. That means being honest, being efficient, not wasting time, being well prepared, being on time, and presenting yourself in a respectable fashion.

Things to Consider: Are you honoring God and the abilities that he has bestowed upon you, whether at your formal place of employment or the place where you volunteer?

The Bible on Work: "Whatever you do, work heartily, as for the Lord and not for men." Colossians 3:23

Even in the hardest circumstances, dreams can give you the courage to live, and I hope I can share that message with children in need. -Kim Yuna

Change is possible. You can do it!

Week #20 Children

Children are the most precious gift on this earth. Children bring meaning to our existence in allowing us to strive to make the world a better place. We have an obligation to ensure the welfare of all children.

The future of humanity is dependent on the assurance that we are bringing up our children in a way that meets their physical, emotional, psychological, and intellectual needs, and equips them for success. All people, and not just parents, have a responsibility to ensure that we are adequately providing the resources needed to mold and form healthy children.

It is important that we allow our children to dream, because without their perspective, we can get stuck in an ideological paradigm that paralyzes us from taking action. It is the dreams of children that breathe life into the world and give hope for a new day.

So let's allow our children to dream, set goals, and grow. Let's encourage them and give them the resources necessary to point them to a path of success.

Things to Consider: When you witness children playing together at a very young age it is obvious that the man-made barriers such as race, socioeconomics, gender, or intellect don't cause them to second-guess the situation. The only thing they care about is having fun.

The Bible on Children: "He called a little child to him, and placed the child among them. 3 And he said: "Truly I tell you, unless you change and become like little children, you will never enter the kingdom of heaven. 4 Therefore, whoever takes the lowly position of this child is the greatest in the kingdom of heaven. 5 And whoever welcomes one such child in my name welcomes me." Matthew 18:2-5

Comparison is a thug that robs your joy. But it's even more than that - Comparison makes you a thug who beats down somebody - or your soul. -Ann Voskamp

Week #21 Comparison

There is not much in our lives that is more dangerous than comparison. It starts in our youth at school and evolves into adulthood with "climbing the corporate ladder".

We have all heard the phrase "keeping up with the Joneses".

We stake our happiness (or illusion of happiness) by evaluating ourselves next to our peers. In doing so, we fall into a trap of this perpetual ever-changing cycle of standards that never fulfills us and leaves us feeling inadequate.

Avoid comparing yourself to others. Everyone is different. Everyone is equal in Gods' eyes. Trying to "keep up" or constantly appraising yourself against others leads to envy or boastfulness, and neither is good.

Be content in who you were created to be. You are uniquely and wonderfully made with your own gifts. If in doing what you were created to do, you do it with all your might – then you are a success. Remember that you were created for a specific purpose, and that purpose wasn't for you to concern yourself with judging whether you are above or below someone else's "level".

Things to Consider: You are perfectly and wonderfully made. If God indeed made you the way you are, then who cares what anyone else thinks?

The Bible on Comparison: "We do not dare to classify or compare ourselves with some who commend themselves. When they measure themselves by themselves and compare themselves with themselves, they are not wise." 2 Corinthians 10:12

No joy can equal the joy of serving others.
-Sai Baba

Week #22 Servitude

I think that when people generally hear the word servitude or servant, their interpretation is skewed by historical definitions of being exploited and oppressed. I believe that servitude can also be a good thing if we humbly look at what it means to serve.

Serving means placing yourself in a vulnerable position to assist or raise up someone else. This is a foreign concept to most Americans, because we are taught to pull ourselves up by our bootstraps and focus on our self-indulgent appetite for "success".

I would argue that living a noble life is not raising yourself above everyone else, but instead raising up others, so you all may better your circumstances together.

"And what do you benefit if you gain the whole world but lose your own soul? Is anything worth more than your soul?" Matthew 16:26

Things to Consider: What if we displayed servitude—within our homes, among family, friends and strangers, and in our places of work—in the same way Jesus did?

The Bible on Serving: "The greatest among you will be your servant." Matthew 23:11

Education is not preparation for life; education is life itself.
- John Dewey

Week #23 Education

The pursuit of knowledge is encouraged and honorable in its purist form—to acquire information. However, knowledge can also blind you from seeing the truth if you allow your perspective and tolerance to make you arrogant and not open to any other views. Receiving knowledge for its intrinsic value it is good and pure. Unfortunately, society is more concerned with the extrinsic values of initials and degrees.

We should daily sharpen our minds to become more refined, moral, and fit for our own sake, not for society's credentials. By becoming more educated, we can truly come to understand who we are and what we were created to do. Seek out wise counsel and allow yourself to be challenged in a pursuit of reaching a more enlightened stage of life.

We were designed with wonderfully intricate minds, and hearts that provide us with countless opportunities to enhance our lives by escaping into the nuances of whatever subject we choose. Find a subject that you want to dive into and become passionate about, while at the same time creating a discipline towards self-education and refining.

Things to Consider: If we used the gifts we have been endowed with, wouldn't that be both rewarding and satisfying?

The Bible on Education: "Let the wise listen and add to their learning, and let the discerning get guidance." Proverbs 1:5

Racial prejudice, anti-Semitism, or hatred of anyone with different beliefs has no place in the human mind or heart.   *-Billy Graham*

Week #24 Culture and Race

It amazes me that since the beginning of time, people have tried to place themselves above each other. This mindset has caused heartache, hatred, and even wars.

I believe that our vast differences in culture, language, tradition and belief only reinforce the beauty of the artistic masterpiece that our creator shaped.

In order to allow the magnificence of our brothers and sisters to enhance our life experience we have to intentionally step out of our comfort zone and form sincere relationships with people who are different from ourselves.

One of life's greatest travesties is that we remain in our man-made silos and fail to appreciate the differences and beauty we all bring to the world. In doing so, we miss the opportunity to share and celebrate each other and our gifts.

Things to Consider: All races and ethnicities are going to populate Heaven because God created everyone. So as Christians how can we justify anything short of equality among all people?

The Bible on Race: "There is neither Jew nor Gentile, neither slave nor free, nor is there male and female, for you are all one in Christ Jesus." Galatians 3:28

Faith is to believe what you do not see; the reward of this faith is to see what you believe. -Saint Augustine

Week #25 Faith

I am a Christian. I believe in the life, death, and resurrection of Jesus the Christ of Nazareth. However, my faith is my own. It is personal. Your faith, whatever it may be, must be your decision. For me, my faith is a relationship. Meaning that through prayer and God's nudging of my conscience, I acquire my calling.

I believe that all of us are the creation of our maker regardless of religious faith or lack thereof. Therefore, I am to commissioned to respect, love, and live in fellowship with people of all beliefs.

Things to Consider: What do you have faith in? Were you raised with any type of beliefs? Do you believe in life after death or do you believe that when we die, we simply expire and cease to exist?

The Bible on Faith: "Now faith is the assurance of things hoped for, the conviction of things not seen." Hebrews 11:1

Vanity is the quicksand of reason. -George Sand

Week #26 Vanity

Vanity seems to me to be a combination of immaturity and insecurity. I admit that when I was young, I struggled a bit with vanity, not because I thought that I was supremely handsome, but because I lacked emotional security within myself.

Don't get me wrong—it's important to take good care of our bodies. But we shouldn't worship them and make them an idol of meaning for our life. Your existence should be deeper that your skin, hair, body make-up, or height.

Things to Consider: Even the old were once young and strong, and everything under the sun goes through seasons of growth until it begins to die.

The Bible on Vanity: "But the Lord said to Samuel, 'Do not look on his appearance or on the height of his stature, because I have rejected him. For the Lord sees not as man sees: man looks on the outward appearance, but the Lord looks on the heart.'" 1 Samuel 16:7

A lot of preconceived notions that I had about fame and status and money and joy and pain, and all of these things that I thought I knew, I didn't. -Alanis Morissette

Week #27 Status

Some people measure their status in life by how much money they make, how great an athlete they are, or how many degrees they have hanging in their office. But the only status you should strive for is being a good person who tries to live a good life.

We all should keep in our minds is that "status" is a state of being, so it is metaphysical instead of physical. Therefore, we are only able to truly reach a greater status through realizing and accepting our own shortcomings. Physical status or belief thereof is a farce and only serves to subject others into a belief of inequality.

Things to Consider: That everyone is the handiwork of our perfect creator, and our creator is perfect. So, if this is true – then we are all the same; no one greater than the other.

The Bible on Status: "Keep your life free from love of money, and be content with what you have, for he has said, 'I will never leave you nor forsake you.'" Hebrews 13:5

I don't want to have lived in vain like most people. I want to be useful or bring enjoyment to all people, even those I've never met. I want to go on living even after my death! -Anne Frank

Week #28 Enjoyment

Enjoy life. Life is going to have hardship, disappointments, and struggles. But remember that circumstances are temporary and times change. Enjoy your life. Love people, and love your family.

In creating an atmosphere of enjoyment in life, remember the word JOY is inside the word enjoyment. Joy is not happiness, getting your own way, or the ability to manipulate life in a way that serves you. Joy stems from being content, at peace, and having an understanding that life doesn't revolve around us or our possessions.

Take time to form meaningful relationships, don't rush life, and learn to have joy in the moment.

Things to Consider: Life is but a glimpse. Our time is short, and so are the moments we share with our loved ones. If this is true – then are we making the most of every moment and enjoying those that are in our company?

The Bible on Enjoyment: "Also that everyone should eat and drink and take pleasure in all his toil—this is God's gift to man." Ecclesiastes 3:13

The purpose of human life is to serve, and to show compassion and the will to help others. -Albert Schweitzer

Week #29 Compassion

I hope your heart breaks for orphans, widows and those who suffer from injustice. It is necessary as part of our humanity to never become hardened to the atrocities that most of the world are subjected to.

It is part of our obligation as fellow humans to develop a heart full of compassion that enables us to use our gifts and talents to positively affect the world.

Things to Consider: Am I a person that has compassion? If so, have I turned that into action, or is it something I internalize and never take the opportunity to help someone in need?

The Bible on Compassion: "Finally, all of you, have unity of mind, sympathy, brotherly love, a tender heart, and a humble mind." 1 Peter 3:8

I don't see success as the goal. Obedience is the goal.
                                        -Jerry B. Jenkins

Week #30 Obedience

It is necessary in our lives to be obedient to the authority of those around us, but we are also commissioned to be obedient to the calling of our life. Obedience is a state of being and doing and it makes its impact on all facets of our lives.

Being obedient enables virtues like humility and discernment to grow within you and help you become more disciplined.

Things to Consider: If we humbly submitted ourselves to be obedient what would we lose other than Pride?

The Bible on Obedience: "Remind them to be submissive to rulers and authorities, to be obedient, to be ready for every good work." Titus 3:1

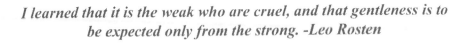

I learned that it is the weak who are cruel, and that gentleness is to be expected only from the strong. -Leo Rosten

Week #31 Gentleness

Be gentle in how you handle life's situations. Allow yourself to be approachable and open to serve those around you. I believe most of life's problems happen because we fail to treat people gently; not physically speaking, but in a way that we can understand and know each other at a deeper level. Being able to positively form relationships through gentleness allows you to let others know that you acknowledge and empathize with them.

Things to Consider: How would our lives be different if we enacted the principle of gentleness? Could or would acting with gentleness possibly change our relationships?

The Bible on Gentleness: "But the fruit of the Spirit is love, joy, peace, patience, kindness, goodness, faithfulness, gentleness, self-control; against such things there is no law." Galatians 5:22-23

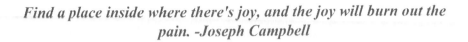

Find a place inside where there's joy, and the joy will burn out the pain. -Joseph Campbell

Week #32 Joyfulness

Joy is a sense of being. It is not a superficial happiness, but a way that you live your life. It is being content with your life's calling and circumstances. It is different than enjoyment in the sense that it is state of being while the other is an act in which you choose to live your life outwardly.

Things to Consider: Are you filled with Joy? Are you peaceful and content as you walk through your journey?

The Bible on Joyfulness: "Rejoice always, pray without ceasing, give thanks in all circumstances; for this is the will of God in Christ Jesus for you." 1 Thessalonians 5:16-18

Modesty is the conscience of the body. -Honore de Balzac

Week #33 Modesty

In living your life, be careful not to draw too much attention to yourself. In some cases, this might mean that you have to humble yourself. In other instances, it might mean giving tribute to someone on your team when you could take credit yourself. Most importantly, modesty is about how you carry yourself.

We should all dress in a way that brings honor to our creator; not in a way that objectifies us as mere physical objects or sexual beings.

Things to Consider: How different would our world be if we showed humility, and modesty? Would there be less objectification of people and things if we presented ourselves in a more modest fashion?

The Bible on Modesty: "Do not let your adorning be external—the braiding of hair and the putting on of gold jewelry, or the clothing you wear— but let your adorning be the hidden person of the heart with the imperishable beauty of a gentle and quiet spirit, which in God's sight is very precious." 1 Peter 3:3-4

Discipline is the bridge between goals and accomplishment.

-Jim Rohn

Week #34 Discipline

Discipline is the state in which we live our lives. It can and should be developed throughout many aspects of our life—how we set goals, how we present ourselves, and how we show honor to others.

Things to Consider: What are the areas of your life that lack discipline? Could you improve your life either personally or professionally by becoming more disciplined?

The Bible on Discipline: "For the moment all discipline seems painful rather than pleasant, but later it yields the peaceful fruit of righteousness to those who have been trained by it." Hebrews 12:11

Life every man holds dear; but the dear man holds honor far more precious dear than life. -William Shakespeare

Week #35 Honor

The Bible teaches us that we are to honor certain people because of their title (e.g. "honor your mother and father...") not because of anything that they have done, but because of who they are.

So hold sacred those you are instructed to honor, not because of our personal feelings or beliefs toward that person, but because some positions should be honored with the respect due to it.

Things to Consider: Have you been good at honoring those around you? How would those close to you, as well as your elders, answer this question in regards to you?

The Bible on Honor: "Honor everyone. Love the brotherhood. Fear God. Honor the emperor. Servants, be subject to your masters with all respect, not only to the good and gentle but also to the unjust. For this is a gracious thing, when, mindful of God, one endures sorrows while suffering unjustly." 1 Peter 2:17-19

I'll take fifty percent efficiency to get one hundred percent loyalty.

-Samuel Goldwyn

Week #36 Loyalty

Do not break the cord of loyalty. If you make a covenant, honor it. Stay true to the contracts that you agree to.

Loyalty is simple in its purest form; it is only after we pervert the word into serving of self-righteous sanctimonious needs that we begin to break this bond.

If you expect others to honor the accords they make with you, then you in turn should take the same care and approach in safeguarding your loyalty to them.

The bond of loyalty is a test of one's character and obedience to the relationships that are formed. Loyalty doesn't necessarily have to be hard work, but it should involve deep consideration, prayer, and meditation.

Things to Consider: Has there been a time in your life where you failed to be loyal? How did that make you feel? How did it make the person to whom you were disloyal feel?

The Bible on Loyalty: "Let not steadfast love and faithfulness forsake you; bind them around your neck; write them on the tablet of your heart." Proverbs 3:3

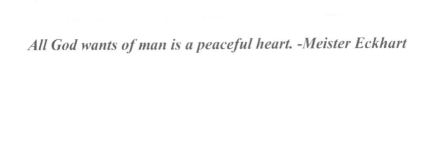

All God wants of man is a peaceful heart. -Meister Eckhart

Week #37 Peaceful

Carry with you a sense of peace that whatever life brings your way it is part of the journey. In having peace within your spirit, you will exude it from your being, allowing those around you to experience it too.

This doesn't mean that peace guarantees a worry-free, unfettered life, but having both spiritual and mental peace will enable you to better deal with challenging situations.

Things to Consider: If we lived our lives in a state of peacefulness do you think that there would be less stress or anger in our lives?

The Bible on Peacefulness: "Do not be anxious about anything, but in everything by prayer and supplication with thanksgiving let your requests be made known to God." Philippians 4:6

Anger and intolerance are the enemies of correct understanding.

-Mahatma Gandhi

Week #38 Understanding

Always seek to understand the events and people around you. In relying on this virtue, you will gain greater insight to those around you as well as the circumstances that are playing out in your life.

One of the grave mistakes that we tend to make as humans is judging others based on our attributes, life experience, capabilities, and resources. Hence, we unfairly burden the "judged" based on an understanding that is foreign to them. How can I judge someone based on an understanding of truth in which I am privy to, but has never served to enlighten their spirit?

Things to Consider: Am I an understanding person? How could I exercise the act of being understanding, and then how would it affect my life?

The Bible on Understanding: "The unfolding of your words gives light; it imparts understanding to the simple." Psalm 119:130

I learned that courage was not the absence of fear, but the triumph over it. The brave man is not he who does not feel afraid, but he who conquers that fear. -Nelson Mandela

Week #39 Courage

Courage is having the ability to know and do the things that are right and just even when those around you are complacent.

Courage is increasingly difficult when we sit parched above others, basking in the comfort and beauty of unchallenged circumstances. In order to truly understand what having courage is, we have to be willing to enter into ourselves in situations, cultures, neighborhoods, and relationships that are not part of our natural comprehension. How can I understand what it is like to be poor if I have never lived poor? Or grasp the reality of malnutrition and hunger if I too have not immersed myself fully into it?

It is easy to empathize with someone, but we cannot truly appreciate the gravity of a situation until we too have experienced it.

Things to Consider: Has there been a time in which you demonstrated courage? What was it and how did it make you feel?

The Bible on Courage: "Have I not commanded you? Be strong and courageous. Do not be frightened, and do not be dismayed, for the Lord your God is with you wherever you go." Joshua 1:9

A day without laughter is a day wasted. -Charlie Chaplin

Change is possible. You can do it!

Week #40 Humor

Humor allows us not to take each other too seriously. We are all wonderfully flawed, and we should take the opportunity to appreciate the humor around us.

This is not an invitation to mock or make fun of one another, as we too have to be cognizant of the great harm we can inflict by doing so.

On the contrary, humor is about seeing the lighter side of life and being able to have fun in both the good and the bad seasons.

Things to Consider: How does it feel when something humorous happens, and you're there to witness it? Or along those same lines, what types of emotions arise in you when you hear a funny joke?

The Bible on Humor: "A joyful heart is good medicine, but a crushed spirit dries up the bones." Proverbs 17:22

Good is positive. Evil is merely privative, not absolute: it is like cold, which is the privation of heat. All evil is so much death or nonentity. Benevolence is absolute and real. So much benevolence as a man hath, so much life hath he.
-Ralph Waldo Emerson

Week #41 Benevolence

Compassion without benevolence is empty. Benevolence is the kinetic action behind our compassion. Benevolence can be as much a physical act as it can be a monetary one.

Regardless of the resources we have, there are still opportunities in which we can serve to be move benevolent.

Things to Consider: If Christians alone were to live more benevolent lives, what type of influence could stem from that? If the Church were to take up some of the "social programs" the government has put in place, could it change the way people think about Christians?

The Bible on Benevolence: "Whoever gives to the poor will not want, but he who hides his eyes will get many a curse." Proverbs 28:27

The supreme good of life is vitality. And vitality is always seeping away. -Roberto Unger

Week #42 Vitality

Live life with energy and passion. Whatever you take on, do it with excitement and using your whole ability.

Whenever we go through the "motions" of completing an act, we are placing our personal stamp of accreditation on it. In various seasons of life, we will have to opportunity to serve in many capacities, but if we do not complete a task or service with full vitality we are basically stating that we stand behind whatever we are doing even if it is not to our full ability.

Things to Consider: Are you serving God with vitality by using the gifts he has bestowed upon you?

The Bible on Vitality: "If we confess our sins, he is faithful and just to forgive us our sins and to cleanse us from all unrighteousness." 1 John 1:9

Let's not forget that the little emotions are the great captains of our lives and we obey them without realizing it   . ⁻
Vincent van Gogh

Week #43 Emotional Intelligence

Seek to understand those around you, and be keen to the emotions of everyone that you interact with. Emotional intelligence is arguably one of the most important traits one should possess in being able to effectively understand those around them.

Be keen to pick up on the nuances of one's actions and words in an ability to form a deeper understanding of who they are as a person and what they value.

Things to Consider: How are you at reading people and understanding their state of being? Do you think by better understanding someone at an emotional level that you could gain a deeper understanding of who that person is and what they value?

The Bible on Emotional Intelligence: "Who is wise and understanding among you? By his good conduct let him show his works in the meekness of wisdom. James 3:13

My best friend is the one who brings out the best in me

-Henry Ford

Week #44 Friendship

Friendship is an act of vulnerability because you're letting another person into your trusted circle and entering into an act of doing life together. Honor your friendships, and be faithful to them.

Without the ability or opportunity to develop friendships, we deny others the chance to know the special qualities we each possess. Likewise, we miss the opportunity to get to know people and share in the possibility of a great friendship.

Things to Consider: Do you have any close friends? How are you at being a friend?

The Bible on Friendship: "This is my commandment, that you love one another as I have loved you. Greater love has no one than this, that someone lay down his life for his friends. You are my friends if you do what I command you." John 15:12-14

Genuine good taste consists in saying much in few words, in choosing among our thoughts, in having order and arrangement in what we say, and in speaking with composure. -Francois Fenelon

Week #45 Composure

Allow yourself to stay in control outwardly even when your inner self is doing back flips.

That is sometimes tough, and it does not mean you should deny how you feel in certain situations. Instead, it means finding ways to make sure that your emotion doesn't control your outward behavior.

Things to Consider: How are you at keeping your emotions under control? Do you scream, yell, and cry until you get your way?

The Bible on Composure: "You will recognize them by their fruits. Are grapes gathered from thorn bushes, or figs from thistles? So, every healthy tree bears good fruit, but the diseased tree bears bad fruit. A healthy tree cannot bear bad fruit, nor can a diseased tree bear good fruit. Every tree that does not bear good fruit is cut down and thrown into the fire. Thus you will recognize them by their fruits." Matthew 7:16-20

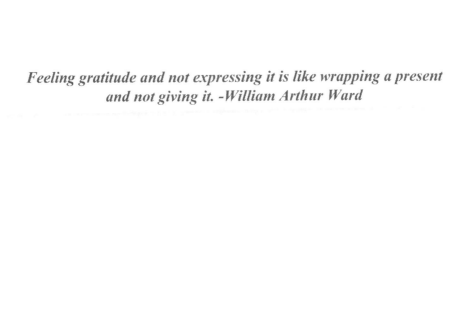

Feeling gratitude and not expressing it is like wrapping a present and not giving it. -William Arthur Ward

Week #46 Gratitude

Be grateful for all things and in all seasons of life. Either with great abundance or lack thereof, be grateful.

Oftentimes we let our circumstances control how grateful we are. But there is always something to be grateful for, whether it be relationships, health, food on your plate, a warm place to sleep, or even the freedom to think differently than those around you.

Things to Consider: Do you have a spirit of gratitude? Do you outwardly give thanks to those who have poured into your life, including our Lord God?

The Bible on Gratitude: "Every good gift and every perfect gift is from above, coming down from the Father of lights with whom there is no variation or shadow due to change." James 1:17

The test of courage comes when we are in the minority. The test of tolerance comes when we are in the majority.
-Ralph W. Sockman

Week #47 Tolerance

Be accepting of people who are different than you to show your humble heart and serving soul.

There is a misconception out there that being tolerant of a person means wholeheartedly agreeing with them. That is not necessarily true, but by being tolerant we can recognize our own idiosyncrasies and imperfections and become more open to the opinions and perspectives of others.

Things to Consider: If we refuse to tolerate those around us even with our imperfections, how then can we then expect others to tolerate us?

The Bible on Tolerance: "Judge not, that you be not judged." Matthew 7:1

Before you speak ask yourself if what you are going to say is true, is kind, is necessary, is helpful. If the answer is no, maybe what you are about to say should be left unsaid.   *-Bernard Meltzer*

Week #48 Helpful

Help those who ask as well as those who don't.

It is easy to help those who are close to us—the ones we have formed relationships with or are our family members. But conversely it is much harder to invest ourselves into a situation or vulnerability we have not previously been a part of.

Things to Consider: What separates humankind from the animal kingdom? As God's creation and the masters of the land don't we have an obligation to help those in need around us?

The Bible on being Helpful: "Do not neglect to do good and to share what you have, for such sacrifices are pleasing to God." Hebrews 13:16

Diligence is the mother of good luck. -Benjamin Franklin

Week #49 Diligence

Be diligent in everything you do to show the care with which you tend to it.

The act of being diligent shows that you took pride and care in whatever you were pursuing. This is greatly important, because by doing so you in turn embed your stamp of approval on the process. Being diligent is more than just the act of doing something, but the thought that supports the act of doing.

Things to Consider: If we are lazy and unwilling to work – is it not our own doing that we may find ourselves in despair?

The Bible on Diligence: "The soul of the sluggard craves and gets nothing, while the soul of the diligent is richly supplied." Proverbs 13:4

He is richest who is content with the least, for content is the wealth of nature. -Socrates

Week #50 Contentment

In all circumstances, be content. Be humbled and accept today what you have been given.

Contentment is realizing that whatever circumstance you find yourself in, you do not have to be defined by it. Instead, you conclude that this is where you currently are and find peace in that.

Things to Consider: If we could be content in any situation, wouldn't life be more fulfilling and not based upon material things?

The Bible on Contentment: "Now there is great gain in godliness with contentment, for we brought nothing into the world, and we cannot take anything out of the world. But if we have food and clothing, with these we will be content." 1 Timothy 6:6-8

True love does not only encompass the things that make you feel good, it also holds you to a standard of accountability.

Monica Johnson

Week #51 Accountability

Allow those around you to challenge you and hold you accountable.

Accountability is a tough one, especially if you fail to allow yourself to form deep and meaningful relationships. Accountability is not passing judgement, but allowing yourself to be challenged by those closest to you, so that you have a deeper understanding of things you might need to change in your life.

Things to Consider: If we as brothers and sisters in Christ have a responsibility to hold each other accountable, shouldn't we help each other to grow in this area?

The Bible on Accountability: "Brothers, if anyone is caught in any transgression, you who are spiritual should restore him in a spirit of gentleness. Keep watch on yourself, lest you too be tempted. Bear one another's burdens, and so fulfill the law of Christ. For if anyone thinks he is something, when he is nothing, he deceives himself. But let each one test his own work, and then his reason to boast will be in himself alone and not in his neighbor. For each will have to bear his own load." Galatians 6:1-5

We should not fret for what is past, nor should we be anxious about the future; men of discernment deal only with the present moment.

-Chanakya

Week #52 Discernment

Study, examine, and show wisdom in all decisions that you make. Have you ever noticed that time brings about discernment? What I mean is, during the "heat" of a moment whatever we decide to do tends to not make as much sense as if we were to wait and process the information before acting or making a determination.

As I get older, and more mature, I find myself not making some of the more rash mistakes I used to. My tongue has become less sharp, and having better judgement has better prepared me to dive into a variety of situations.

I am certainly not saying that I have mastered discernment, as I admit I am still working hard to be a better judge of things.

Things to Consider: Being able to determine right from wrong is the basis for all virtues. How can there be a "right" or a "wrong" without the ability to determine what is actually right or wrong?

The Bible on Discernment: "For the word of God is living and active, sharper than any two-edged sword, piercing to the division of soul and of spirit, of joints and of marrow, and discerning the thoughts and intentions of the heart." Hebrews 4:12

About the Author:

John F. Hendershot is a husband, father, businessman, leadership expert, and speaker. He holds a Bachelor of Arts in Public History, a Master of Science in Management, and a Master in Business Administration.

Mr. Hendershot currently serves as the CEO of DIG-IT, INC. a utility, telecommunications and pipeline contractor based in Michigan. He is also the current President of the Great Lakes Trenchless Association. Over the years, Mr. Hendershot has held positions on a number of non-profit and municipal boards.

Mr. Hendershot and his family reside in beautiful Holland, MI on the shores of Lake Michigan (well, a few miles away from the shores).

Thank you for taking the time to read my thoughts. I hope that this book has challenged your thinking and inspired personal growth. Remember that life is a journey — things are not always easy, lovely, or jovial. Most of us have had some terrible experiences, major letdowns, not to mention sleepless nights, heartache, and even trauma. The good thing is that none of those moments define our entire life, but they are necessary steps in our overall journey.

People can change. You can change, and I can change, and that is the goal every day of my life – to work on the less desirable things about myself and become a better person.

God Bless you on your journey. Keep your faith and never give up on yourself.

-JFH

*NOTE: If you are challenged spiritually - I encourage you to surrender your life to Jesus Christ – if you are not ready for that; that's okay too. Seek out a local bible believing church and ask to be paired up with a mentor that can assist you in growing your faith, and walk alongside of you in your journey.

Made in the USA
Middletown, DE
22 March 2017